JIM BRANDENBURG

Sand and Fog

ADVENTURES IN SOUTHERN AFRICA

Edited by
JOANN BREN GUERNSEY

WALKER AND COMPANY NEW YORK

First published in the United States of America in 1994
by Walker Publishing Company, Inc.; first paperback edition
published in 1996

Published simultaneously in Canada by Thomas Allen
& Son Canada, Limited, Markham, Ontario

Library of Congress Cataloging-in-Publication Data
Brandenburg, Jim.
     Sand and fog : adventures in southern Africa / Jim Brandenburg ;
  edited by JoAnn Bren Guernsey.
        p.   cm.
     ISBN 0-8027-8232-9 (cloth). —ISBN 0-8027-8233-7 (lib. bdg.)
     1. Namibia—Juvenile literature.   2. Namibia—Pictorial works—
  Juvenile literature.   3. Natural history—Namibia—Pictorial works—
  Juvenile literature.   [1. Namibia—Description and travel.
  2. Natural history—Namibia.]   I. Guernsey, JoAnn Bren.   II. Title.
  DT1523.B73   1994
     968.81—dc20   93-30425
ISBN 0-8027-7476-8 (paper)   CIP
                                                          AC

Book design by Victoria Hartman

Printed in Hong Kong

10 9 8 7 6 5 4 3 2 1

Contents

Chapter 1

A DESERT QUEST

There was sand everywhere, an impossible amount of sand covering thousands of square miles and heaping into dunes as high as 1,200 feet. The ultimate sandpile. It was uniformly fine and found its way into everything. I blinked sand from my eyes, blew it from my nose, spit it from my mouth and throat. And I tried in vain to protect my photographic equipment from it. The wind blew, but the landscape contained no trees, wires, or anything else for the wind to blow through and produce its expected howl. What I heard was the hiss of shifting sand.

It was in this moonscape setting that I found myself on a quest for a particular photograph. I wasn't even certain what it was I was looking for, only that I'd probably know it if I saw it. At times it seemed I was on the trail of a unicorn because the animal I was tracking had the same mystical quality about it. And my quest in the Namib desert of South-West Africa appeared, at times, to be nearly as futile.

The oryx—usually referred to in Namibia as a gemsbok—is a nomadic creature, almost as large as a horse and with long, sharp, unicornlike horns. The Namib offers only an occasional tuft of desert grass and no fresh water that I could see. In tracking small

Oryx easily traverse the dunes of the Namib, often keeping to the firmer sand on windswept ridges.

Facing page: Ocean-driven air currents create elegant shapes on the massive dunes.

A moonscape scene — thousands of square miles of sand in the Namib.

Facing page: Climbing a sand dune is a struggle — take three steps forward and slide two back.

herds of oryx for hours on end, I saw their lonely wandering search for food and water, up and down the dunes endlessly.

At times I wanted nothing more than to give up, to retrace my steps and crawl into my tent. Nothing is more exhausting than climbing sand dunes. So much of the time I found myself helplessly sliding backward. Three steps forward, two steps back, leg muscles burning. Sinking into the sand past my ankles, my progress undone by the miniature sand avalanches under my feet.

The oryx, with their four agile feet, had a distinct advantage over me with my clumsy two. They could stroll away from me in the most casual way. But I learned to see in their tracks where even they'd had trouble negotiating deep sand and where, at the firmer, windswept ridges of the dunes, they (and I) could then find easier footing. Of course, they weren't encumbered as I was by backpack and heavy photographic equipment, but at least I carried water with me. Where was their water, their food?

The oryx appeared almost healthy, considering their environment, but I was in Namibia during a drought and many animals were, in fact, dying. At one point in my quest, I found an oryx skeleton half buried in the sand. The horns were magnificent—black, ridged, slightly curved, and over three feet long. I managed to bring them back with me, and they still adorn a wall in my home.

An oryx skull is a reminder of the harshness of several years of drought.

Other pictures I had seen of this creature in the desert drew me into this quest. Many images occupy my mind in this way, from other photographers' failed efforts. It's like someone else has taken notes for me, left clues for me to follow. With the right lighting, the right composition, what a stunning photograph could result! The other oryx pictures I had seen were portraits of the animal, but I was after something more.

I'd seen the animal, and I'd seen the sand—two simple elements of nature—and I wanted to combine the best of each to make a unique statement about survival, about the incredible ways animals adapt to even the harshest habitat. In addition, I felt lighting was critical. Shadows would help me to reproduce the melancholy, otherworldly quality of the dunes and the ghostlike presence of the animals.

In addition to the oryx skeleton, the sand held other surprises for me, more encouraging evidence of adaptation and escape strategies. I uncovered a sand lizard and grabbed it, only to find the tail broken off in my hand. This natural form of self-protection allowed the lizard to scurry away and, eventually, to grow a new tail. A large white spider and I startled each other; she instinctively curled up her legs to go cartwheeling down the dune away from me. I saw many different mounds in the sand—moving ones—and for the most part I chose to leave these alone.

A lizard avoids predators and the hot midday sun by burying itself in the cool sand.

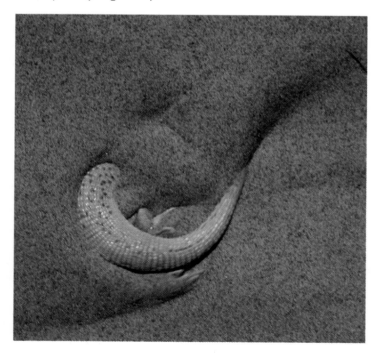

Facing page: Abstract patterns on the sand are evidence of varying wind directions.

I spent almost three weeks, off and on, trying to get the oryx shot I wanted, and most of the time I felt totally defeated. It's all too rare for even the best wildlife photographers to actually get the images they're after. I wish I could pinpoint some precise moment when I triumphed over the odds. It was late afternoon and the lighting was perfect. One animal separated itself from the others. But the *art* of photography is not really clear to me while I'm trying to capture specific images. What I am most aware of is the act of forcing myself into a situation and then going on automatic, shooting frame after frame. What I remember is the quest.

Oryx will travel for miles to find a small patch of grass.

8

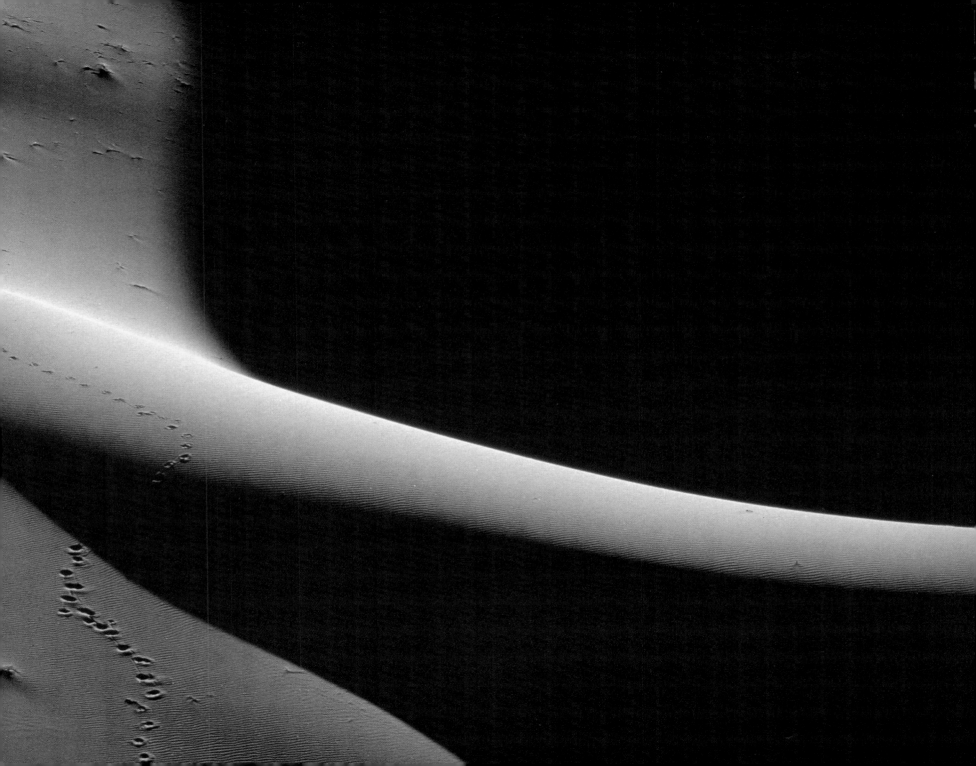

South African soldiers on night patrol.

The children of war at a school for the disabled. These children were injured when they found and accidentally set off unexploded weaponry.

Chapter 2

LAND OF CONTRASTS AND SURPRISES

All the while I was pursuing my ideal images, I knew I was supposed to be taking other kinds of pictures for the *National Geographic.* My assignment was not to explore the mysteries of nature but to record the ravages of war and racial hatred.

Namibia (formerly known as South-West Africa) lies directly northwest of South Africa—the country infamous for its apartheid system of white minority rule—and Namibia has had to fight long and hard for its freedom from South African control. *National Geographic* sent writer Bryan Hodgson and me to cover the political and racial tensions occurring at the time. The voting populace of Namibia, which is mostly black, has recently taken control of the country, but at the time I left on this assignment, Namibians were very much at war.

Namib means "place of no people," but this country is hardly that. It is the home of several distinctive ethnic groups, each with its own culture and history. Along with indigenous Africans we found many white descendants of German, Afrikaner (Dutch),

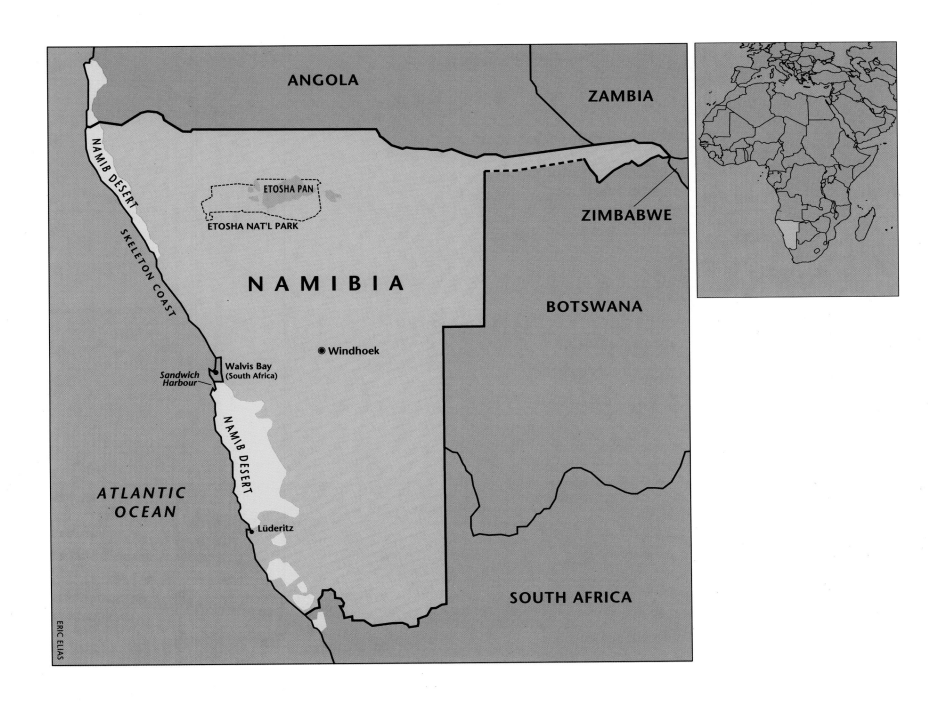

ANGOLA

ZAMBIA

ZIMBABWE

NAMIB DESERT

SKELETON COAST

ETOSHA PAN

ETOSHA NAT'L PARK

NAMIBIA

BOTSWANA

●Windhoek

Walvis Bay
(South Africa)

*Sandwich
Harbour*

NAMIB DESERT

ATLANTIC
OCEAN

●Lüderitz

SOUTH AFRICA

ERIC ELIAS

Kung men hold an all-night dance, creating their own music with singing and drumming.

Old German stores on Windhoek's main street.

and English settlers, and people of mixed descent. It was a land that defied generalizations. While in the thriving and surprisingly modern capital city of Windhoek (complete with shopping malls and high-rise buildings), an anthropologist told us, "We speak twenty-seven different languages and dialects in Namibia. You shouldn't expect us to speak with a single voice."

Living on the edge, this Ovahimba man has learned to survive in the barren land of rock and sand near the Skeleton Coast.

Disembarking from the plane in Windhoek, I was, frankly, scared. This was not exactly my kind of story. But I was at a stage in my career that when the *Geographic* said to go somewhere, I went. It was my first chance to do an international, rapidly unfolding political story. As a *Geographic* editor has since pointed out to me, however, I tend to turn every assignment into a natural history story. In the great Namib Desert how could I resist?

After fulfilling my official obligations to provide images of war and of the racial conflicts involved, I turned, as quickly as possible, to the region itself. What captured my imagination was the delicately balanced ecosystem of the Namib Desert. Stretching along 1,300 miles of the Atlantic coast, the Namib appears to be barren wasteland but is actually a habitat for creatures that exist nowhere else on earth.

Facing page: Fog rolls in from the cold ocean current at Sandwich Harbour.

Coastal rock formations on the southern tip of the Namibian coast near Oranjemund.

⌒ *Chapter 3*

A SEA OF DUNES

H ow does life exist in the Namib Desert? The answer lies in the winds and in the sea. And, ultimately, the ecosystem depends upon, of all things, fog.

The perpetually blowing winds are called "Soo-oop-wa" in one of the local languages. For countless centuries they have blown, modeling the vast sea of dunes into ever-changing linear waves, ridges and hollows, and cliffs of cascading sand. But the winds are more than just the sculptors of the Namib. For part of the year a hot, dry wind blows from the east bringing food—a scattering of organic particles from which desert plants draw nourishment. At other times, warm Atlantic winds join forces with the cold current from Antarctica. The winds, charged with moisture, roll in to lay a clammy shroud of fog over the coastal desert.

It may not rain in this region for years, so the dense fog (which appears about one morning in every five) is the desert's only regular form of precipitation. Plants and animal life of the Namib have evolved in incredible ways to use these meager amounts of moisture in the form of mist or dewdrops.

Facing page: Most life forms on the dunes receive moisture only from the fog.

Ridges carved by wind cast shadows in the setting sun.

Even beetles have evolved to survive in this harsh climate.

The oryx I tracked drew nourishment *and* water from the desert grass and its precious burden of dew. Somehow, this is usually sufficient. An oryx is also remarkable for its ability to withstand the intense desert heat. Its body temperature rises so high that its blood could destroy the animal's brain cells. But, in a unique adaptation, blood destined for the brain is first cooled by circulating through a network of capillaries in the oryx's nasal passages.

At least oryx can, and do, migrate to grassier regions. What about those creatures trapped in the desert?

They have evolved licking rather than drinking, as moisture beads up on plants, sand, even on the creatures themselves. The palmetto gecko (a type of lizard), for instance, licks moisture from its lidless eyes. And tiny black beetles stand almost on their heads, motionless on dune ridges, waiting for water droplets to accumulate on their bodies. Then, slowly, this moisture trickles down the insect's grooved back into its mouth.

A lizard inspects a drift of windblown plant material for insects.

Later in the day when the fog has lifted, these creatures, like most in the Namib, escape the heat by digging into the cool depths of the sand. The sidewinding adder finds not only coolness in the sand but also camouflage. This snake, which efficiently travels sideways across the hot, loose sand, lies in wait for prey, totally buried except for its eyes, which are set high on its head.

One of the more remarkable adaptations to desert dryness can be seen in the sand grouse. To fetch water for his chicks, the male parent flies up to fifty miles to a water hole, collects moisture in its thick breast feathers, and flies back. The waiting chicks then eagerly sip water from these still-wet feathers. This is only one of the daily miracles occurring in the region.

The sand grouse has a unique ability to use its breast feathers as a sponge to transport water great distances.

Chapter 4

EXPLORING THE COASTAL DESERT

The delicate colors of the flamingo enhance the otherwise stark beauty of the Namib coast.

Facing page: The author's camp on the Skeleton Coast. The Land Rover carried gear over hundreds of miles of sand dunes.

We did most of our travel across the desert in a Land Rover, the classic mode of transportation in Africa. Travel in a Land Rover is not unlike a bone-jarring ride in a buckboard wagon. The vehicle could take us anywhere, but it did, occasionally, get stuck in deep sand. Then we'd have to let half the air out of the tires for better traction.

Naturally we carried all of our fresh water with us. My main concern was that we had drinking water; I didn't give much thought to water for bathing. It wasn't terribly hot most of the time we were there. In fact, we had to wear heavy clothing to protect us from the damp chill of early morning and late evening.

The starting place for much of my wildlife photography, including my pursuit of the oryx, was a place known as Sandwich Harbour. It is a reed-fringed lagoon that has become partially separated from the ocean. Sweet water seeps in from beneath the dunes and sustains the greenery, thus providing a rich breeding ground and sanctuary for many animals. This is a magical place where sharks swim right offshore and hundreds of flamingos

An unsuspecting flamingo is no match for the fleet-footed jackal.

stroll along the beach. When the flamingos venture into the dunes themselves, they are pursued and caught by jackals, who then run around with the pink-feathered bodies dangling from their mouths.

Farther north, we explored the Skeleton Coast. Fierce storms have, for centuries, caused shipwrecks along this part of the Namib. The Skeleton Coast has been a particularly treacherous region for ships not only because of the storms but also because of currents, the fog, and the lack of safe harbors. Shifting sands alternately cover and uncover such wreckage as masts and railings. Some ghost ships are still trapped in rocks offshore; a few others can be seen mired in sand as far inland as a mile!

Facing page: Flamingos crowd the lagoon at Sandwich Harbour.

A casualty of the fog-draped Skeleton Coast.

But the name of this region refers not to the skeletons of old galleons and clippers washed ashore but rather to the human bones littering the beach. People aboard those ships may have survived the wrecks, but they could not survive the desert awaiting them. After staying close to the ship for shelter, they inevitably died, and their bones joined the skeletons of whales and other unfortunate creatures.

As I walked along the beach, I was struck by how undisturbed it was. The region is too remote for local people to visit and was at that time not open to outsiders. We were among the first Western journalists in modern times ever to be allowed on the Skeleton Coast. It was here that I saw many bizarre sights, most of them too far off in the distance or too fleeting for a good photograph. I saw elephants sliding down sand dunes. I saw where a lion, absurdly out of place, had caught a porcupine right there on the

A pride of lions living in the dunes.

An unlikely scene — giraffes with no trees.

The eerie figurehead of an old sailing ship washed up on the Skeleton Coast.

beach. And I saw giraffes wandering over the sand with no tree in sight for them to munch on.

But one of the most memorable moments for me came when I stumbled across an eerie figurehead from some long-lost vessel. About the size of a watermelon, its facial features had been worn

Jim Brandenburg photographs a dance.
(© Annie Griffiths Belt)

A Himba woman wearing a traditional mixture of ocher and fat.

nearly blank by windblown sand. Still, there seemed to be an expression of utter despair etched in that wood, and, against the backdrop of rocks, fog, and sea, it provided one of my better photographs.

Although the Skeleton Coast seemed to speak so eloquently of despair, further exploration of the northern part of Namibia supplied me with many other images, and these were not of death but of life. Many of the country's diverse ethnic groups live in areas to the east of the northern coast, in the desert plains where sand gives way to gravel.

I vividly remember one night with a group of people known as the Himba, who lived not far from the Skeleton Coast. The Himba often covered themselves, head to toe, in red ocher mixed with animal fat. During my visit it appeared that the women did all the work while the men sat around the fire, gossiping and complaining.

The interesting thing is that, overworked though they might be, it was the women who seemed to me vibrant and happy. They did a lot of clapping and dancing, and at one point I joined them. It is obvious from a photo I took of one of the Himba men, not long after the dance, how the men viewed my intrusion. If looks could kill . . .

I took some of my favorite photographs in a Herero town where the women wore magnificently colorful dresses and turbans. The style was originally introduced by the wives of missionaries, anxious to make the local women cover their bodies with more than

If looks could kill . . .

A Herero woman in her everyday clothing.

29

Herero priest blessing the people.

Years of practice allow this Herero woman to carry items as heavy as this sewing machine on her head.

A bird's-eye view of Ovambo houses.

just ocher and beads. But the Herero then went on to develop a style distinctly their own.

It was also with the Herero that I witnessed a group baptism. One of the local priests was surrounded by about thirty people from the community. They were kneeling, and he walked among them, drinking and spitting water on them; in this way he baptized them all at once.

The Ovambo communities of the north are the largest and most powerful in Namibia. Here they far outnumber all other ethnic groups combined. I visited an Ovambo community where the houses were arranged in a complex maze of hidden chambers, dead ends, and narrow passages designed to baffle would-be intruders.

31

At the opposite end of the coastal desert, in the south, we were surprised to find the richest diamond mines in the world. The Diamond Coast is officially off-limits to unauthorized visitors. But our association with the *National Geographic* apparently meant we were to be trusted, even in this forbidden region. Security near the diamond mines is amazing; we had to endure full-length body X rays each time we were about to leave.

The diamonds on this coast come from prehistoric times, weathered from numerous volcanoes more than a hundred million years old, and gathered by an ancient network of rivers for a

Facing page: Coastal diamond-mining site.

When a diamond is found, it is inserted into a locked sizing box.

Inspecting the day's diamond harvest.

A fur seal uses a rock as a chin rest as it basks on the beach.

Facing page: Seals surfing where the waves break onshore.

journey toward the sea. Over millions of years the sea worked and reworked the diamonds, concentrating them and destroying inferior stones. What was left were gem diamonds of incomparable quality. Stormy surf deposited them with gravel in ocean bedrock and in layers on the beaches.

I will never forget my visit to a sorting house, sitting at a table heaped with gems of every shape and color imaginable, playing with them as though they were simply sparkling pebbles. In fact, one pile was worth millions of dollars.

Not far from the diamond mines, near Lüderitz, we were able to see more examples of animals seemingly out of place in the desert. In fact, many animals depend on the extraordinarily rich sea life in the cold waters of the Atlantic. I was enchanted by a throng of penguins waddling around. One of my strangest photos is of

*Jackass penguins find shelter
in an abandoned house.*

penguins congregated in a long-abandoned house on an island. And I was able to watch seals surfing, a sight that scientists say is quite rare. But by this point, nothing about Namibia would have surprised me.

Jackass penguins test their nests on Halifax Island.

⟨⟩ *Chapter 5*

THE ETOSHA PAN

Etosha" has many meanings, but one Ovambo described it best as "the place of dry water," referring to the frequent mirages. These liquid illusions dance above the surface of a dry lake bed known as the Pan. I spent about two weeks in Etosha, one of the world's greatest national parks, larger than the state of Massachusetts and located in the north-central part of Namibia.

Most of the year there is not a drop of rain. But underground reservoirs sustain some water holes in the region all year round, attracting a fantasyland of wildlife: zebras, lions, cheetahs, leopards, giraffes, elephants, springbok, wildebeest—a photographer's dream.

When the rains come, they continue for about three months. Water begins to fill the Pan, flowing into its natural depression from all directions. A vast, shallow lake is formed, about fifty miles across but barely two feet deep. Thousands of flamingos settle on its surface, appearing as if from nowhere, overnight. Millions of catfish become feasts for egrets and herons.

Facing page: Kudus and zebras at an Etosha water hole.

Wildebeest and springbok search for water during the dry season at Etosha Pan National Park.

Springbok and waterfowl at a water hole.

Karakul lynx licks its lips in satisfaction after finishing a meal of sand grouse.

I was struck by the sight of a flock of ostriches and the spectacular sunrise behind them. In my photos, their necks look almost fluorescent. The problem was to shoot this photo fast enough, while the sun was still little more than a sliver. Otherwise the brightness would overpower the scene. Looking through a long lens, it's amazing how fast the sun rises — it practically shoots up — and I had time for only ten to fifteen frames. Luckily, it was enough.

During this rainy season, most animals enjoy a bountiful time; they are strengthened and renewed, prepared for the long, harsh months ahead.

Facing page: Ostriches glow in a sliver of light for a few moments at sunrise.

After the rains end, the Pan first becomes mired in soggy clay. Then it hardens under the harsh Etosha sun into a deep pattern of cracks. Herds of animals move on for fresh grazing, a mass migration triggered each year by the long dry season. Many animals travel 100 miles and more, following trails leading from one water hole to the next. At each water hole, predators wait, and it becomes more and more dangerous to seek water. In spite of the formidable protection provided by their mothers, young zebras, wildebeest, and springbok fall prey to cheetahs and lions.

A peaceful scene at a water hole is instantly transformed into a roar of hooves and splashing water when a lioness appears. Elephants are among the few animals who come fearlessly to water; but, if they have a very young calf with them, even elephants get edgy when a lion or other predator appears.

Facing page: Elephants gather at a shrinking water hole.

The sun filters through dust stirred by wary zebras at a dried-up water hole.

The area grows hotter and dryer by the day. The winds stir up a haze of dust and sand, making the whole area look as if it's smoldering. At sunset, when elephants give themselves dust showers to repel insects, they appear to be surrounded by flames.

At last, thunder rolls across the bleached plains of Etosha National Park, and the endless cycle of predator and prey, death and renewal continues.

An Etosha elephant rids itself of insects with a dust bath.